The Maya

Tamra Orr

Watts LIBRARY™

Franklin Watts
A Division of Scholastic Inc.
New York • Toronto • London • Auckland • Sydney
Mexico City • New Delhi • Hong Kong
Danbury, Connecticut

Note to readers: Definitions for words in **bold** can be found in the Glossary at the back of this book.

Photographs © 2005: Bridgeman Art Library International Ltd., London/New York: 42 (Giraudon/Biblioteca Nacional, Madrid, Spain); Corbis Images: 47 (Richard A. Cooke), 34 (Freelance Consulting Services Pty Ltd.), 3 right, 12 (Kimbell Art Museum), 4 (Otto Lang), 50 (Daniel LeClair/Reuters), 20 bottom (Danny Lehman), 38, 43 (Charles & Josette Lenars), 25 (Buddy Mays), 40 (Enzo & Paolo Ragazzini); Corbis Sygma/Sergio Dorantes: 49; Justin Kerr: 8, 9 (Rollout Photograph K555); Peter Arnold Inc./Martha Cooper: 21, 28; The Art Archive/Picture Desk: 3 left, 22, 30, 36 (Dagli Orti), 24 (Dagli Orti/Archaeological and Ethnological Museum, Guatemala City), 44 (Dagli Orti/Biblioteca Nacional Mexico), 19 (Dagli Orti/Museo de America, Madrid), 29 (Dagli Orti/Rijksmuseum voor Volkenkunde Leiden (Leyden)); The Image Works: 27 (ARPL/Topham), 14 (Rob Crandall), 20 top (Macduff Everton), 48 (Bill Lai), 11, 18 (The British Museum/Topham-HIP); Woodfin Camp & Associates/Robert Frerck: 33, 37.

Cover illustration by Gary Overacre

Map by XNR Productions Inc.

Library of Congress Cataloging-in-Publication Data

Orr, Tamra.
　　The Maya / Tamra Orr.
　　　　p. cm. — (Watts library)
　　Includes bibliographical references and index.
　　ISBN 0-531-12296-4 (lib. bdg.)
　　1. Mayas—History—Juvenile literature. 2. Mayas—Social life and customs—Juvenile literature. 3. Mayas—Antiquities—Juvenile literature. 4. Mexico—Antiquities—Juvenile literature. 5. Central America—Antiquities—Juvenile literature. I. Title. II. Series.
F4134.M39 2005
972.81—dc22

2004025232

Contents

Chapter One
Creation and the Gods 5

Chapter Two
A Continuing Puzzle 15

Chapter Three
A Period of Change 23

Chapter Four
Reaching the Peak 31

Chapter Five
Creating the Mystery 39

Chapter Six
Struggling for a Future 45

52 **Timeline**

53 **Glossary**

56 **To Find Out More**

60 **A Note on Sources**

61 **Index**

Q'ukumatz was one of the creators of the world according to Maya myth and is depicted as a feathered serpent. This feathered serpent sculpture was found on a building at Chichén Itzá.

Chapter One

Creation and the Gods

Many cultures have at least one version of a creation myth. How did the world begin? How was it made? For the Maya, it all started with Q'ukumatz (ku-ku-maats), the feathered snake who lived in the water, and Juraqan (who-ra-kahn), who lived in the sky. Before the world began, there was nothing but endless sea and empty sky. It was completely silent. Then the Two Creators, Q'ukumatz and Juraqan, appeared and cried out:

Thus let it be done! Let the emptiness be filled!
Let the water recede and make a void.
Let the earth appear and become solid.
Let it be done.
Thus they spoke.
Let there be light, let there be dawn
in the sky and on the earth!
There shall be neither glory nor grandeur
in our creation and formation
until the human being is made, man is formed.
So they spoke.

Thus, creation had begun. Mountains burst out of the waters. Trees and plants sent their roots deep into the soil. Animals of all shapes and sizes were created. However, when these animals did nothing but make noise instead of praising their creators, Q'ukumatz and Juraqan knew their job was not finished yet. The world needed human beings.

They molded the first people from clay. They quickly found that these clay people had no minds of their own, so the first people were destroyed. Next, the Creators made people out of wood, but they soon realized these wood people had no hearts or blood. They were dry. They were without tears, smiles, souls, or respect for their gods, so they were destroyed. Heavy rains came and brought a flood and carried them away.

The Creators said, "Let human beings appear who will praise us." They called on the fox, coyote, parrot, and crow to bring them corn from the mountains. Grinding the corn to powder, they made the next form of human being. Adding water for blood, they were pleased with this new species except for one thing. These human beings were too knowledgeable. They seemed to be able to see everywhere and understand everything. Didn't this mean they were equal to the gods? The Creators asked the Heart of Heaven to cloud these people's eyes so they would not know so much. The Creators also asked that the people have shorter life spans and less intelligence so that the people could never compete with the gods. It was done, and humankind was born. According to the *Popol Vuh*, this is how the world and its very first Maya people began.

The Hero Twins

The largest part of the *Popol Vuh* consists of an epic story about the Hero Twins, Junajpu (hoo-nah-POOH) and Xbalanque (sh-bah-LAHN-kay). These two young men were humans with godlike powers. Their father, Jun Junajpu, was also a twin. He and his brother, Wuqub' Junajpu, were

ballplayers who had been killed by the cheating death gods in Xibalba (shee-bahl-BHA), the watery underworld. When the Hero Twins were grown, they followed in their father's footsteps and went to meet the death gods. In the underworld, the gods tried repeatedly to trick Junajpu and Xbalanque, but the twins were too clever. They passed safely through tests in the House of Gloom, the House of Knives, the House of Cold, the House of Jaguars, and the House of Fire. However, in the House of Bats, Junajpu, seeking shelter with his blowgun, peeked out to see if the danger had passed. As he peeked, a bat

This is a scene from the Popul Vuh and shows the underworld.

flew over and took off his head. His brother made him a temporary new head out of a gourd and amazingly, Junajpu could still see and talk!

The Hero Twins played the ballgame with the death gods using Junajpu's real head for the ball. Xbalanque then switched his brother's head for the gourd, angering the death gods. Finally, the twins allowed themselves to be killed because they knew the gods demanded a sacrifice. Their bones were ground into powder and then tossed into the river, where they were reborn first as catfish, then as fishermen.

Maya Gods

While the Maya believed in almost two hundred different gods, they felt all of them came from one primary spiritual force. Some of the most important gods were:

Itzamnaaj	God of gods, of writing, of curing, of divination, and of day and night
Chaak	God of rain and lightning
K'inich Ajaw	God of the sun
Pawahtun	Earth-bearer god
Yum Kax	God of corn and maize
Yum K'imil	God of death, also known as Ah Puch
Ixchel	Goddess of fertility and childbirth
Ek Chuah	God of merchants

Although in human form again, the twins appeared somewhat different. They were dancing beggars who performed tricks so amazing that word soon spread about them. Finally, the disguised twins were summoned to a command performance for the gods in Xibalba. They sacrificed a dog and brought it back to life. Xbalanque cut off Junajpu's head and brought him back to life. Soon, the death gods begged to be killed so the twins could bring them back to life too. The twins obliged for the first part. They killed the gods and then left them that way, finally triumphing. In return, it says in the *Popol Vuh*, the twins rose to the heavens and became the sun and the moon.

The Spiritual Life of the Maya

The Maya lived as partners with their many gods. They felt deeply connected to the different **deities** (gods or goddesses) and believed that if they praised them and lived as they commanded, the gods would meet all the Maya's earthly needs. The

A stone panel shows a Maya noble named Lady Xook having a vision of a serpent after performing a bloodletting ritual.

Maya thought that if they offered the gods food and praise through offerings and sacrifices, the gods would ensure that the sun rose each day and that the rain would come, allowing for new life and growth. They also believed that when each person was born, an identical soul was placed in the body of an animal. This animal companion spirit was known as *nagual*. Whatever happened to one would happen to the other. A person could transform into the shape of his or her animal companion spirit during war, in a dream, or in a spiritual vision.

The Maya communicated with their gods through prayer, visions, and **bloodletting** sacrifices, or purposeful

11

Captives (lower left) are presented to a Maya ruler (right). For special occasions, they might be killed as sacrifices to the gods.

cutting of the skin to shed blood. Any time there was an important occasion, such as a birth or death, bloodletting would play a part. When a new heir was born to a king, the king would sacrifice his own blood to the gods in gratitude. In addition, visions were a part of the bloodletting rituals. It was through these visions that one could speak to or contact his or her ancestors or gods. The act of bloodletting represented the most precious gift one could give the gods. Maya art often portrays a person having a vision with the Vision Serpent rearing up over his or her head, which symbolized the contact between the natural and the supernatural world where the gods lived.

For some events, the Maya would offer food or incense to the gods. For special events, such as the naming of a new king, Maya kings would let their own blood and perform human sacrifices. Those sacrificed were primarily captives taken in raids against their neighbors.

Birth of the Sun

The Maya believed that the sun set each night and descended into the underworld. It was then reborn the next morning.

While archaeologists have been able to learn some things about the Maya, many questions about their culture remain unanswered.

Chapter Two

A Continuing Puzzle

The ancient Maya continue to intrigue and puzzle experts the world over. Much of what surrounds this unique group of people is still a complete mystery. Even after thousands of excavations, little is known about many aspects of ancient Maya culture, from its very beginnings to its virtual disappearance. No researcher or archaeologist can point to the exact origin of the Maya. All they can do is look at the clues left behind and create likely possibilities. Many of them agree

This map shows the traditional
homelands of the Maya.

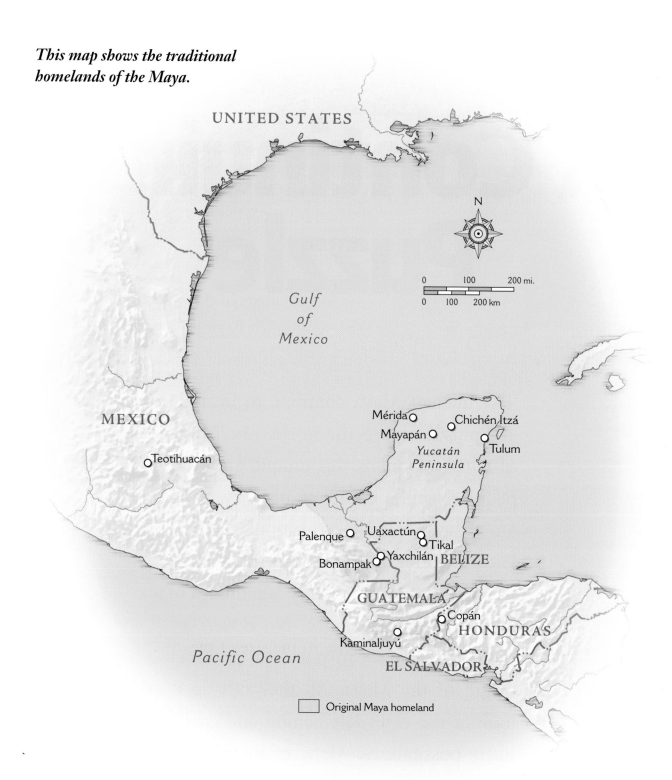

UNITED STATES

Gulf
of
Mexico

N

| 0 | 100 | 200 mi. |
| 0 | 100 | 200 km |

MEXICO

Teotihuacán

Mérida   Chichén Itzá
Mayapán   Tulum
          Yucatán
          Peninsula

Palenque   Uaxactún
           Tikal
Bonampak Yaxchilán BELIZE

GUATEMALA

Copán
HONDURAS
Kaminaljuyú

Pacific Ocean

EL SALVADOR

☐ Original Maya homeland

The Maya in Mesoamerica

The Maya lived in two different regions in Mesoamerica. These areas are known as the Maya Highlands and the Maya Lowlands. The highlands were mountainous terrain in what is now southwestern and southern Guatemala. The lowlands, which were located in Mexico, Belize, northern and central Guatemala, and Honduras, contained relatively flat or level ground.

There are two seasons in Mesoamerica. The rainy season lasts from about mid-May to November. The dry season begins in December and ends in May. Farmers have to time their planting carefully.

that roughly 10,000 to 15,000 years ago, the ancestors of the Maya traveled from Siberia to Alaska over the frozen **Bering Strait**. Arrowheads found in caves in Central America date back at least 10,000 to 12,000 years. Some experts think that the ancestors of the Maya were of Asian origin. They came to this conclusion based on body characteristics shared by both groups, including limited height, scarce beard, eyelid folds, and black, straight hair.

Wherever they first came from, the Maya settled in areas throughout modern Guatemala, Belize, El Salvador, Honduras, and the Mexican states of Yucatán, Quintana Roo, Tabasco, Campeche, and Chiapas. Today this area is called Mesoamerica, and it stretches across roughly 125,100 square miles (324,000 square kilometers), or close to the size of the state of New Mexico.

The earliest inhabitants of Central America hunted such animals as woolly **mammoths** and **mastodons**. Once these animals became extinct, these people turned to hunting

Slash and Burn

The Maya used a simple method of clearing land for farming called slash and burn, which involved cutting down and burning sections of forest. The ashes enriched the soil, which helped fertilize the crops.

jaguars, deer, pheasants, pumas, toucans, iguana, and squirrels. They also caught seafood, such as fish, oysters, turtles, and snails. They hunted with many different types of tools, ranging from nets, ropes, and slings to spears, bows, and arrows.

The early Maya lived in caves, rock shelters, and open camps. As time went on, however, the Maya began to shift from being hunters and gatherers to being farmers. They began to settle in small farming villages with homes. To make their homes, they would cut down young trees, strip the bark, and place them atop a stone foundation. They would fill in the spaces with more young trees or with a plaster called **stucco**. The roofs were made of palm thatch and two doors were built right across from each other to allow for optimal airflow. They would often build three or four homes around a central area in the middle. This cluster of homes is called a **compound**.

Each home might house several related adults, including several generations from babies to grandparents. Each one of them had his or her own responsibilities to take care of over the course of the day. Women would stay in the compound, tending to chores ranging from preparing food, tending the fire, and collecting firewood to repairing tools, making pottery, and sewing clothing. The men would spend their days out in the fields, taking care of the crops.

The Maya grew corn, which was the base of their diet, as well as beans, chili peppers, sweet potatoes, and squash. They also planted various fruit trees near their villages. Their focus on growing

As corn was one of their most important crops, the Maya worshipped a special corn god.

successful crops brought their attention to the seasons and how the weather affected them. This awareness of the changing of weather patterns would eventually result in the Maya's intense interest in both calendars and astronomy.

The Olmecs

Many researchers believe that the Maya, along with later Mesoamerican groups, were strongly influenced by another successful group of people called the Olmecs. Living in the area of what is now Veracruz, Mexico, the Olmecs created one of the first Mesoamerican societies with a focus on agriculture. They had gods, chiefdoms, and a wide trading network. They created huge stone monuments. The Maya would adopt and expand on these elements within their own society. The Olmecs also created the concept of the pyramid in Mesoamerica. The Maya would later refine the technique, adding more complex rooms and intricate designs.

The Beginning of Chocolate

Maya royalty were one of the first groups of people to eat chocolate. They drank it unsweetened in a liquid form they called the drink of the gods. *Kakaw* was the Maya term for chocolate.

In fact, the Olmecs are often said to have created the **template**, or pattern, that many other cultures in the region would

The Maya were inspired by the pyramids of the Olmecs and built their own versions of these structures. This pyramid is located in the Maya city of Chichen Itzá.

follow. The Olmecs developed the first notion of the calendar, which the Maya expanded, creating a calendrical writing system. The Olmec society thrived from 1500 to 100 B.C. However, by 700 B.C., many of their cities, including the central city of San Lorenzo, were abandoned, and their religious altars destroyed. By 100 B.C., the last of the Olmec culture had disappeared, and no one knows the reasons why.

At about this time, the Maya began to develop into one of

This building is believed to have been used as an observatory by the Maya. They studied the stars, the moon, and the planets.

The Skill of Pottery

Pottery making was one of the Maya's top skills. Pottery vessels were used for cooking and storing food and also played an important role in religious rituals. The Maya made most of the vessels out of clay coils that were smoothed together. They did not have the potter's wheel or any other machinery but their hands.

The Maya would often decorate the pottery using a substance called slip paint. It was a mixture of finely ground pigment, clay, and water. They would use the paint to put drawings and hieroglyphs on the vessels. Amazingly enough, some of the pots they made were as tall as an adult human.

the most successful and inventive cultures ever stemming from Mesoamerica. Not only would they grow to a size of more than two million people but they would also discover profound concepts about their world, including the motion of stars and planets, the notion of time, the idea of the number zero, and the development of a written language.

These are the ruins of an observatory in the city of Peten from the Preclassic Period.

Chapter Three

A Period of Change

The next period of Maya history is called the Preclassic Period. It stretched from approximately 1800 B.C. to A.D. 200. As the Maya continued to settle into regions of Mesoamerica and develop their farming abilities, changes began to occur in their society. These changes allowed their society to become more stable. Cities spread out into the lowland forests and into the highland mountains. Four-house compounds expanded into sprawling square plazas. The Maya even created

The Maya preferred an elongated skull as shown in this close-up on a Maya painting.

reservoirs to hold rainwater to provide drinking water through the dry season for their growing population.

New traditions formed as the society grew. A class system developed, with clear differences between the nobility and the commoners. The nobles lived in large palaces made of stone. Commoners lived in smaller homes with thatched roofs.

The Look of the Maya People

Because they worshipped Yum Kax, the corn god, the Maya felt it was attractive to look something like an ear of corn. To do this, they would place the skulls of their newborns between two boards to reshape them into long and backswept heads. Because an infant's skull is soft, this didn't cause any pain. The Maya also liked the appearance of slightly crossed eyes, so they would hang a ball of resin or wax in front of their children's eyes in the hopes that it would cause their eyes to cross and stay that way.

Adult Maya would often wear jewelry made of jade. Men would sometimes tattoo their hands, faces, and torsos, and women had tattoos from the waist up. Many of them had pierced noses, lips, and ears. Clothing was of little importance

Divine Jade

Jade was considered to be divine by the Maya. The green color of this beautiful gemstone was similar to the color of corn stalks and symbolized rebirth and renewal. The Maya wore jade in everything from earplugs to chips between their teeth.

to commoners and they often wore very little. Men would wear simple loincloths. Women would wear woven **huipils**, which were similar to ponchos and were brightly colored and decorated with designs.

When boys were toddlers, they would have white beads put into their hair. The beads would remain there until the child reached **puberty**, or began maturing into a young adult (usually around twelve or thirteen years old). Then the beads would be removed in an official ceremony called the Descent of the Gods. The teenager would go to live in a separate house with other unmarried boys his age until he turned fourteen. At that point, he was considered to be ready for marriage.

A Maya girl went through a coming-of-age ritual as well. She wore a red shell in her belt until the ceremony, at which time it was removed. This young girl, usually about twelve years old, would then be taught how to cook and clean.

A young man's family hired a professional matchmaker called an *atanzahab* to find the right wife for their son. Maya couples didn't marry for love. They married whomever their parents decided was a proper match. Often, they would already be married before they would have the chance to speak to their spouses for the first time. The atanzahab would make sure that the couple's names and horoscopes went well together and then negotiated a price for the girl. She also would bargain with the girl's parents on how long their new son-in-law would have to work for them. The typical time was between five and seven years, during which the couple shared the girl's parents' home. Women were only allowed one husband, but men were allowed more than one wife. Because there was no emotional bond between couples when they married, divorce and second marriages were common. A man who didn't like his wife also had the option of simply leaving her family if he had been married for less than one year.

Putting It in Writing

One of the Maya's most impressive contributions to the world was the development of a hieroglyphic writing system capable

Inventing the Wheel

One of the Maya's many inventions was the wheel. Because of the rough terrain and lack of horses in their land, it was used only for children's toys.

of recording their spoken language. During the last part of the Preclassic Period, they invented a complex system of hieroglyphs, which are painted or drawn symbols that represent specific words or actions. Only the temple priests were taught how to read and write using this system. Maya scribes carefully recorded many details of the lives of kings and their achievements. They also wrote many almanacs describing the movement of the planets and stars in bark-paper books known as **codices**. Writing would eventually be used in temples and on the walls and stairways of their pyramids. These writings commemorated important events, such as births, deaths, battles, and sacrificial rites.

In addition to writing, the Maya also developed the concept of zero in figuring their mathematics. This idea had escaped many other cultures. Furthermore, by watching the changing of the seasons and the constellations closely, they created the first true calendars.

Although the ancient Maya civiliza-

The Maya Codices

In the 1500s, the codices of the Maya were burned by the Spanish because the books were thought to be the work of the devil. Only four of the books survived the destruction. They are known as the Madrid Codex, the Dresden Codex, the Paris Codex, and the Grolier Codex.

A Sense of Time

The Maya were very interested in the passage of time and were very aware of the motion of the planets, the stars, and the moon. They believed that time moved in cycles. Events were seen as cyclical, meaning that they repeated. For the Maya, there was a specific time for everything. Based on math and astronomy, they developed the *Tzolk'in*, or "sacred" calendar, and the *jaab*, or solar calendar. The tzolk'in year consisted of 260 days, or *k'in*, and each day was associated with a certain god or goddess. The jaab year, or *tun*, was 365 days long, divided into eighteen months or *winal* of twenty days each and a brief five-day period at the end known as *wayeb*. This short month was considered unlucky and so was a time of sacrifice, fasting, and rest.

The Maya were active traders and wanted such goods as jade, shell, and obsidian

tion was not yet at its peak of growth, by 300 B.C. it had already established a trading post at Kaminaljuyu in the highlands of Guatemala. They had many different things to trade, including jade, obsidian, flint, cacao beans, spices, sea salt, animal pelts, bird feathers, wood, and pottery. These items were exchanged for various services within their own communities' markets as well as in area fairs and trade centers.

The next period of Maya history was a time of extraordinary growth and war. Together, this expansion and fighting would bring both positive and negative changes.

The Leyden Plaque

The Leyden Plaque, a large piece of jade shaped like a rounded rectangle, was discovered in 1864 and is dated A.D. 320. It would have been hung with others from a ruler's belt and was meant to clang together, creating a beautiful sound.

Palenque is one of the important cities of the Classic Period of Maya history.

Chapter Four

Reaching the Peak

The Maya culture reached its peak in the era known as the Classic Period. It lasted from about A.D. 250 to roughly 900. Trade centers were thriving. Cities were growing at an amazing speed, and more than sixty different city-states emerged, each one ruled by its own king. The Maya people differed from most others in that they were never ruled by just one supreme leader. Of course, this didn't mean the different kings respected each other's territories. This entire period was full of constant battles between regions, and alliances changed frequently. Battles were fought over trade routes, farmland, and access to natural resources.

One of the most powerful cities in the Maya region was Tikal, located in central Guatemala. This city covered more than 6 square miles (2.3 sq km). At its peak, it had more than three thousand buildings, including everything from temples and pyramids to shrines and houses. The city was a major religious center where people came to pay homage to the gods. As many as 50,000 people lived in Tikal at its peak, and it developed a strong trade relationship with the Central Mexican city of Teotihuacán, Mesoamerica's greatest city. Another large city in the southwestern region of Mesoamerica was Palenque. At different times in its history, at least two women ruled the city. Copán was the ruling city in the southeastern Maya area.

Human-Made Mountains

Construction never seemed to stop in these expanding cities. The Maya were able to build enormous cities because of the abundance of natural resources available to them. Although the Maya had no metal at all to use, they created monuments and buildings using tools made from flint, obsidian, and granite. They constructed pyramids, or human-made mountains, to honor both their kings and their gods. The higher they could make them, the closer they felt they were to their gods. Some reached more than 200 feet (61 meters) in height.

Workers would chip away at a huge block of stone to

remove a slab. Then they would brush and chip the sides of the slab until it was fairly smooth. After that, they would carry these massive stones from the quarry to the pyramid construction site on their backs or by rolling them on logs. They didn't have any pack animals, such as mules or horses, to help them. Other parts of the pyramids were made from a combination of water, soil, clay, grass, and pieces of pottery. Through a complicated process of burning **limestone**, the Maya had also figured out how to make a type of stucco mortar to hold things together, to pave floors, and to create sculptures. The outside of the pyramid was usually painted red.

The Maya built their pyramids to become closer to their gods.

33

An Early Skyscraper

Teotihuacán's Pyramid of the Sun, built in A.D. 225, was the largest stone pyramid in all of pre-Columbian America. It measured 738 feet (225 m) on each side and stood 213 feet (65 m) tall. That is as tall as a twenty-story skyscraper!

Excavations around the pyramid have found a tunnel-like cave underneath it. At the end of the cave, experts discovered a set of chamber rooms in the shape of a clover leaf. It was thought to have been used for fire and water rituals.

The color red symbolized that the building was a gift to the gods. Many buildings also featured carved images of the gods.

The two basic types of pyramids are called platform pyramids and temple pyramids. The platform pyramid is flat on top and was probably used as a stage for rituals. The temple pyramid, which could have one or more staircases, once had a structure at the top.

Unlike the pyramids of ancient Egypt, Maya pyramids were not usually used as burial chambers. The tombs that have been found at or near the pyramids mostly contain the remains of sacrificial victims. The elite were often buried in their own carefully built tombs in residential areas. Commoners were usually in the floors of the main living areas of their homes. Before being placed in the ground, their mouths were filled with ground corn or jade beads to ensure the safe passage of their souls into the underworld.

Win or Else!

Almost every Maya city featured a ball court. Shaped like a capital *I*, it ranged in size from a volleyball court to a football field. A certain ball game was played regularly there, but the rules of the game are still not completely understood. A heavy ball made of solid rubber was used. As large as a modern basketball, it bounced quite high. Similar to soccer, players could only use their shoulders, upper arms, thighs, and hips to hit the ball. Players wore padding to keep from being injured. Experts believe this game was similar to the game the legendary Hero Twins played with the death gods while they were in the underworld. The major difference between this ball game and most games, however, was that it was not played for recreation. Instead, it was a battle, often between two

Let's Play

Maya game boards were scratched onto the floors of stone buildings. A favorite game was pattoli, which was played with burnt grains of corn. Players moved these game pieces from square to square as in modern board games.

This is a ball court used by the ancient Maya.

city-states that had just gone to war. The losing city's team was expected to play, and should it lose, its members were forced to make the ultimate sacrifice. Their team was killed when the game was finished.

During the Classic Period, every resident of a city-state was kept busy with one job or another. Women still tended their homes, using corn to make a huge variety of meals from corn cakes to tortillas. Men worked the fields, planting corn and other crops, while many other people labored on various building projects. Others within the community worked on

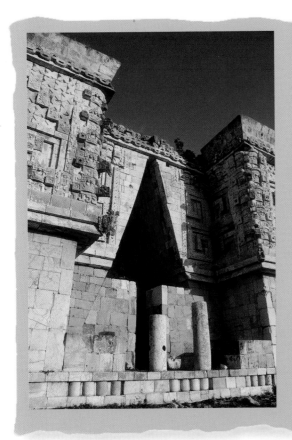

Unique Architecture

Some Maya buildings have an interesting architectural element called a corbelled arch. The arch is formed by pushing stone blocks out from each side of a wall until they met in the middle.

crafts, such as spinning and weaving cloth for the commoners, dying fabric for the nobles, making pots for different uses, and performing repairs on homes, tools, and canoes.

Looking at the Maya culture during these years, it would have been almost impossible to imagine that it would all be gone in only a few centuries. What would be even harder for experts to understand is why this thriving culture would disappear so mysteriously.

*The city of **Tulum** was active during the Postclassic Period of Maya history.*

Chapter Five

Creating the Mystery

Picture these bustling Maya cities that for centuries had been filled with the sounds of workers chipping flint at stones, farmers making their ways through fields, and religious figures murmuring religious rituals now gradually going silent. After enjoying decades of prosperity and growth, the time of the Maya was about to take an unexpected turn. From about A.D. 910 to 1524, called the Postclassic Period, cities were abandoned and a culture was lost.

During the Postclassic Period, the city of Tikal became deserted.

The changes began in the central and southern sections of Mesoamerica. Construction stopped, trading slowed down, and religious and political centers faltered. One by one, the Maya cities fell into disrepair and soon after, were totally abandoned by their residents. For example, the once-powerful Tikal was defeated by the city-state of Caracol in 562, laid almost **dormant**, or completely quiet, for a century, and then was revived by a new ruler. By about 889, this new government had also fallen apart. The city was deserted, as was Palenque. Many of the cities on the Yucatán Peninsula in the north flourished in the wake of the central region's collapse. However, they too would begin to collapse by the beginning of the eleventh century.

Just after A.D. 1000, a group of Maya warriors and

merchants from the Tabasco region of Mexico came to the northern area with the intention of taking control of the existing trade routes and land resources. One group set up a capital city at Chichén Itzá and kept control of it for two centuries. Another city was created west of Chichén Itzá called Mayapán. In the early thirteenth century, the leader of Mayapán conquered Chichén Itzá. Soon this area was the leading power in the Yucatán. It retained its importance for almost 250 years, before it too fell. Almost all of the Maya cities were quiet and empty by the 1500s.

Researchers have come up with a variety of explanations for this period of decline. Some believe that there was an agricultural crisis, such as a drought. Others think the decline was due to the military invasions of other city-states. Still, others believe it was famine, disease, or overpopulation that caused the collapse of Maya society.

By the thirteenth century, the only place the Maya were still flourishing was in the northern Yucatán Peninsula. This is an area in southeastern Mexico that separates the Caribbean Sea from the Gulf of Mexico. It continued to be a vibrant and stable area until the early 1500s and the arrival of the Spaniards.

Invasion from a New Direction

In 1502, the explorer Christopher Columbus's ship came across a Maya trading canoe near the Gulf of Honduras. Columbus could tell that it was a trading canoe and wanted to know more about the culture it came from. The Spaniards took the traders' canoe and their goods, including axes, pottery, and cacao beans. It wasn't long before the word spread about the prosperous Maya. For the next three centuries, Europeans would continue to come to Mesoamerica to take much of what the Maya had.

In 1517, the Spanish explorer Francisco Hernández de Córdoba came to the Maya area searching for gold and glory and to spread Christianity. It wasn't long before the Spanish and the Maya went to war. In 1562, tragedy befell the Maya. Friar Diego de Landa, the Yucatán bishop, had befriended a Maya chief. The chief had shown Landa a vast storage of sacred codices. Landa was so shocked at the religious beliefs detailed in the books that he immediately burned all of them.

The arrival of the Spanish forever changed the lives of the Maya.

Next, he went on a three-month crusade to force the Maya to accept Christianity and turn away from their native religion. He proceeded to burn virtually every manuscript the Maya had, as well as to torture many Maya. By 1564, the Maya in the Yucatán were conquered, but still the fighting continued. The Maya held on for more than 150 years. In the end, they lost the struggle because the Spaniards had horses and guns and had brought European diseases against which they had no natural immunity. The last Maya city near Lake Petén Itzá fell to the Spanish in 1697.

The Maya had no choice but to accept both Christianity and Spanish rule. In doing so, they gave up much of their own culture and traditions. More than fifty thousand Maya had died, either in battle, from starvation, or from the diseases the Europeans had brought with them. They were forced to work as slaves to the Spaniards. Over time, Maya cities were covered up in rain forest growth, not to be rediscovered for centuries.

An Island's Treasure

Off the coast of the Yucatán Peninsula is a small island called Jaina. At the end of the Maya Classic Period, large tombs were built there, filled with decorations and treasures that the dead would need for the afterlife. Excavations uncovered hundreds of clay figurines measuring less than 12 inches (30.5 cm) tall. Most are of nobles with very detailed facial expressions. Researchers suspect that these figures depict actual people.

This illustration is one of the many drawings of Maya ruins done by Frederick Catherwood.

Chapter Six

Struggling for a Future

In the early 1800s, people around the world wanted to know much more about these exotic lands of Mesoamerica. Two of these people were the popular travel writer John Lloyd Stephens and the artist Frederick Catherwood. Stephens, sometimes called the "father of Maya archaeology," had heard stories of the lost civilization in the Yucatán and wanted to see its ruins for himself. He invited his friend Catherwood to join him, and they set off in 1839. Over the next few years,

Cruz Parlante

In 1847, during the Caste War, the Maya were forced back into the forests around Quintana Roo. When they were about to give up, they received divine inspiration. According to legend, a talking cross, or *cruz parlante*, rose up from the ground and began speaking, encouraging them to keep fighting. Today, the area where this is said to have occurred is a shrine with three wooden crosses. Volunteers in the area keep watch over the shrine. The location of the original cross is kept secret for protection.

they would work together to produce travel books about the wonders they found. Catherwood's drawings were so detailed that they almost appeared to be photographs, and they amazed readers the world over.

The living conditions for the surviving Maya during this time, however, were still quite poor. In desperation, they rose up and rebelled against the Mexican government, demanding better treatment. The Maya asked for some of their land back and the end to slavery. Called the **Caste** War, the battle lasted from 1847 to 1901 and is considered to be the most successful Indian rebellion ever fought in North America, even though the Maya did not officially win. The word *caste* means "social class" or "position." The Caste War got its name from the fact that the peasants rebelled against the upper classes and the government.

In 1915, the Mexican military finally gave Chan Santa Cruz city to the Maya, and the Maya proceeded to set up small villages there. Within a decade, slavery was over, and the

Mexicans began to support the Maya by helping them start their own farms.

The Modern Maya

Today, many of the Maya's cultural traditions mirror the traditions of their ancestors. Many farmers live in thatched-roof houses and work their fields every day, while women stay at home and cook, clean, and weave. Most of these Maya are Catholic, but they find a way to blend their new religion with their culture's old traditions. The Christian God is referred to as Our Father Sun. The Madonna is referred to as Our Mother Moon. The symbol of the cross represents Christianity, yet it also is considered a sacred, ancient symbol to the Maya.

There are more than six million Maya living in Belize, Mexico, Guatemala, and Honduras today. Many of them

An Annual Celebration

Each year, the Mexican city of San Juan Chamula holds a five-day long festival, known as the Festival of Games, to celebrate its Maya roots.

There are more than six million descendents of the ancient Maya living in Mexico and Central America today.

A Shirt's Message

Many modern Maya women wear huipils, which are blouses designed with special patterns showing what Maya group or town they come from.

continue to struggle to have a comfortable life. Beginning in 1954, a civil war in Guatemala cost the lives of more than 100,000 Maya and exiled more than 1,000,000 Maya from their homes. Thousands simply disappeared, and more than four hundred villages were completely destroyed. Tens of thousands fled the area in hope of finding a peaceful life elsewhere. More than one million came to the United States.

Even though the war ended with a truce in 1996, many of the Maya in Guatemala continue to be persecuted. Still, others live in poverty and suffer from malnutrition.

A quarter of the modern Maya are **illiterate**, or unable to read. Despite this, they keep working toward finding a comfortable balance between the traditions of their ancestors and their present conditions. People such as Rigoberta Menchú Tum, a Guatemalan woman, are helping them. Menchú Tum won the Nobel Peace Prize in 1992 for her fight to help the Maya. She watched many members of her family die struggling for their freedom in Guatemala, and was also threatened when she spoke out. In 1981, she fled to Mexico for her own

Rigoberta Menchú Tum (center) has worked tirelessly to improve the lives of modern Maya.

A Remote Discovery

Arthur Demarest, an anthropologist from Vanderbilt University, explores remote areas of the world that others have not dared to investigate. In September 2000, Demarest discovered a 27,000 square-foot (2,508.4 sq m) Maya palace deep in Guatemala. Three stories high, the palace has more than 170 rooms, plus eleven courtyards. It was found in the ancient city of Cancuén, or Place of Serpents. Its name still rings true. The place is full of snakes. It was also covered in vegetation and is the site of one of the last large tropical rain forests left in southern Guatemala. The palace is home to endangered species such as the howler monkey and woolly anteater, as well as artifacts and treasures dating back to the sixth century A.D. The excavation will continue for years. Demarest hopes the site will eventually become an ecotourism center that will help preserve and protect the Maya culture.

safety and there she wrote her autobiography. Winning the Nobel Prize helped bring the plight of today's Maya to people's attention, and Menchú Tum hopes that that will make a difference. As she puts it, "We are not myths of the past, ruins in the jungle or zoos. We are people and we want to be respected, not be victims of intolerance and racism." The Maya have a very rich heritage, and with enough support and compassion, perhaps a bright and hopeful future as well.

Timeline

10,000–12,000 B.C.	Arrowheads are discarded in Mesoamerican caves.
1500 B.C.	The Olmecs began creating a culture.
700 B.C.	The Olmec city of San Lorenzo collapses.
600 B.C.	Tikal is first settled.
300 B.C.	The Maya establish a trade center.
100 B.C.	Olmec civilization disappears.
1800 B.C.–A.D. 200	The Preclassic Period of Maya civilization occurs.
C. A.D. 320	The Leyden Plaque is created.
C. A.D. 200–900	This is the Classic Period of the Maya.
562	Tikal is conquered.
900–1524	The Postclassic Period of Maya civilization occurs.
1502	Columbus spots the first Maya people.
1517	Córdoba comes to the Maya region.
1520	Spanish soldiers conquer the Guatemalan Maya.
1697	The last Maya city collapses.
1839	Catherwood and Stephens take their first trip to the Yucatán Peninsula.
1847	The Caste War begins, and the talking cross appears.
1901	The Caste War ends.
1915	The Mexican government returns Chan Santa Cruz to the Maya.
1954	The Guatemalan Civil War begins.
1996	The Guatemalan Civil War ends.

Glossary

atanzahab—a Maya professional matchmaker or person who matches up couples for marriage

Bering Strait—a narrow stretch of water separating Alaska from Siberia and connecting the Arctic Ocean with the Bering Sea

bloodletting—purposeful cutting of the skin

caste—a system of social classes in which people are separated from others through the distinctions of hereditary rank, profession, or wealth

codices—handwritten books

compound—a building or buildings, especially homes or groups of homes, set off and enclosed by a barrier

deities—gods and goddesses

dormant—a period of hibernation or stillness

huipils—Maya clothing worn by women and resembling ponchos or capes

illiterate—unable to read or write

jaab—Maya solar calendar

k'in—a day in the Maya calendar system

limestone—stone made from seashells and coral

mammoth—a large, hairy, extinct elephant

mastodon—any of several very large, extinct mammals resembling the elephant but having molar teeth of a different structure

nagual—the Maya spiritual animal companion

pattoli—popular Maya board game

puberty—the physical change from childhood to young adulthood

reservoirs—hand-dug pits or pools that hold water

resin—wax

stucco—a type of hard finish for outside walls, usually made out of cement, sand, and lime, and applied while wet

template—pattern

tun—a year in the Maya solar calendar

Tzolk'in—the Maya sacred calendar

wayeb—the five days at the end of each Maya year

winal—the Maya equivalent of a month

To Find Out More

Books

Baquedano, Elizabeth. *Eyewitness: Aztec, Inca and Maya.* Australia: DK Publishing, 2000.

Braman, Arlette. *Secrets of Ancient Cultures: The Maya: Activities and Crafts from a Mysterious Land.* Indiana: John Wiley & Sons, Inc., 2003.

Coulter, Laurie. *Secrets in Stone: All About Maya Hieroglyphs.* Ontario: Little, Brown and Company, 2001.

Day, Nancy. *Your Travel Guide to Ancient Mayan Civilization.* Minnesota: Runestone Press, 2000.

Fisher, Leonard E. *Gods and Goddesses of the Ancient Maya.* New York: Holiday House, 1999.

Galvin, Irene Flum. *The Ancient Maya*. New York: Benchmark Books, 1996.

Garcia, Guy. *Spirit of the Maya: A Boy Explores his People's Mysterious Past*. New York: Walker and Company, 1995.

Green, Jen, et al. *The Encyclopedia of the Ancient Americans: Explore the Wonders of the Aztec, Maya, Inca, North American Indian and Arctic Peoples*. London: Southwater Publications, 2001.

Kirwan, Anna. *Lady of Palenque, Flower of Bacal, Mesoamerica, A.D. 749*. New York: Scholastic Press, 2004.

Macdonald, Fiona. *Step into the Aztec and Mayan Worlds*. London: Lorenz Books, 1998.

Takacs, Stefanie. *The Maya*. Danbury, CT: Children's Press, 2004.

Organizations and Online Sites

Arte Maya Tz'utuhil
http://www.artemaya.com
This site features the biographies and artwork of artists from the Highlands of Guatemala.

Copán Museum, Honduras
Museo Popol Vuh, Guatemala City
http://www.maya-archaeology.org/museums/copan/copan.html
This web address takes you to the home page of the Copán Museum, which has an extensive Maya collection. A link on the home page will take you to the Museo Popol Vuh, another Maya museum with a large collection.

Maya Folktales
http://www.folkart.com/~latitude/folktale/folktale.htm
This site features five different Maya folktales translated into English by Fernando Peñalosa.

Maya Ruins
http://mayaruins.com
This site takes the viewer on a photographic tour of Maya sites in the Yucatán Peninsula. There are twenty-two different locations to click on and learn about.

McClung Museum
http://mcclungmuseum.utk.edu/specex/maya/maya.htm
This site from the McClung Museum shows the large collection of Maya artifacts that it had on display in January of 1999.

Mostly Maya
http://www.mostlymaya.com/
This site has links to many helpful sites.

Mundo Maya

http://www.mayadiscovery.com

This is the home page for the online version of the *Mundo Maya* magazine. It features articles on Maya history, crafts, legends, archaeology, and daily life.

Rabbit in the Moon

http://www.halfmoon.org

This fun and brightly illustrated site features information on using Maya calendars to calculate dates, creating Maya models, reading hieroglyphs, and much more.

Science Museum of Minnesota

http://www.smm.org/sln/ma/

This site features a number of photographs of Maya sites, as well as activities. It also allows viewers to take an interactive Maya adventure.

A Note on Sources

Researching information about the Maya was a trip through history for me. Their rise to power and mysterious disappearance was like a mystery without a solution. For the most accurate and fascinating information, I depended a great deal on Michael Coe's *The Maya* and Lynn Foster's *Handbook to Life in the Ancient Maya World*. I also found a great wealth of information about the current status of today's Maya on the Internet. I even consulted Cherry Hamman's *Mayan Cooking: Recipes from the Sun Kingdoms of Mexico* to get a stronger feel for the culture. It was Frederick Catherwood's unbelievable paintings of his journeys into Maya regions, however, that made the time period and the environment become real in my mind. They were so detailed and accurate that I felt like I could fall into them and live among the Maya for a while. What questions I would ask if that happened!

—*Tamra Orr*

Index

Numbers in *italics* indicate illustrations.

Ah Puch. *See* Yum Kimil.

Archaeology, *14*, 15, 17, 43, 45, 50, *50*

Astronomy, 19, *20*, 21, *22*, 27, 28

Atanzahab (matchmaker), 26

Ball courts, 35, *36*

Bloodletting sacrifices, 11, *11*, 13

Calendars, 19, 20, 27, 28

Cancuén (city), 50

Caracol (city-state), 40

Caste War, 46

Catherwood, Frederick, *44*, 45–46

Chak (god of rain and lightning), 10

Chan Santa Cruz (city), 46

Chichén Itzá (city), *4*, *20*, 41

Children, 24, 25–26

Chocolate, 19, *19*

Christianity, 42, 43, 47

City-states, 31, 36, 40

Class system, 24, 46

Classic Period, *30*, 31–32, 36, 43

Clothing, 24–25, 48, *48*

Codices, 27, *27*, 42

Columbus, Christopher, 41

Corbeled arches, 37, *37*

Córdoba, Francisco Hernández de, 42

Corn, 18. *See also* Yum Kax.

Crafts, 37

Creation myth, *4*, 5–7

Cruz parlante (talking cross), 46

Deities, 10, 11, 32
Descent of the Gods cere-
    mony, 25–26
Diseases, 43

Ek Chuah (god of mer-
    chants), 10

Farming, 17, 18–19, 23, 36,
    39, 47
Food, 36

Hero Twins, 7, 8–11, 35
Hieroglyphics, 26–27
Houses, 18, 23, 47
Huipils (clothing), 25, 48, *48*
Hunting, 17–18

Itzamnach (god of gods),
    10
Ixchel (goddess of fertility
    and childbirth), 10

Jaab (solar calendar), 28
Jade, 24, 25, *25*, *28*, 29, *29*
Jewelry, 24, *25*
Jun Junajpu (father of Hero
    Twins), 7–8
Junajpu (Hero Twin), 7,
    8–11

Juraqan (creator), 5–7

Kakaw (chocolate), 19, *19*
Kaminaljuyú (city), 29
Kings. *See* Rulers.
K'inich Ajaw (god of the
    sun), 10

Landa, Diego de, 42–43
Leyden Plaque, 29, *29*

Marriage, 26
Mayapán (city), 41
Men, 18, 24, 47
Menchú Tum, Rigoberta,
    49, *49*, 51
Mesoamerica, 17
Mexico, 46–47

Naqual (animal companion
    spirit), 11

Observatories, *20*, *22*
Olmec culture, 19–20

Palenque (city), *30*, 32, 40
Pattoli (game), 35
Pawahtun (Earth-bearer
    god), 10
Peten (city), *22*

Platform pyramids, 34–35
Popol Vuh ("Council Book"), 7–11, *8–9*
Population, 21, 47
Postclassic Period, *38*, 39–41, *40*
Pottery, 21, *21*, 37
Preclassic Period, *22*, 23, 27
Pyramids, *14*, 19, *20*, 32–35, *33*, *34*

Quintana Roo (city), 46
Q'ukumatz (creator), *4*, 5–7

Religion, *4*, 5–11, *8–9*, *18*, 21, 39, 42, 43, 47
Rulers, *12*, 31

Sacred calendar, 28
Sacrifices, 11, *11*, *12*, 13
Slash and burn farming, 17
Slavery, 43, 46
Solar calendar, 28
Spain, 27, 41–43, *42*
Sports, 35–36, *36*
Stephens, John Lloyd, 45–46

Temple pyramids, 34, 35
Teotihuacán (city), 32, 34, *34*

Tikal (city), 32, 40, *40*
Tombs, 35, 43
Trade, *28*
Tulum (city), *38*
Two Creators, 5–7
Tzolk'in (sacred calendar), 28

Underworld. *See* Xibalba.

Vision Serpent, 13

Weather, 17, 19
Women, 18, 47, *47*, 48
Writing system, 20, 21, 26–27, *27*
Wuqub' Junajpu (uncle of Hero Twins), 7–8

Xbalanque (Hero Twin), 7, 8–11
Xibalba (underworld), 8–9, *8–9*, 10, 13, 35

Yum Kax (god of corn and maize), 10, *18*, 24. *See also* Corn.
Yum Kimil (god of death), 10

About the Author

Tamra Orr is a full-time writer living in Portland, Oregon. She is the author of almost fifty nonfiction books for children and families, including *The Parent's Guide to Homeschooling, Native American Medicine*, and *School Violence: Halls of Fear, Halls of Hope*. She also writes for multiple national publications and several educational-testing companies. She has a Bachelor of Science degree in both secondary education and English from Ball State University in Muncie, Indiana. She is a mother of four (ages 8 to 20) and loves to read, stare at the mountains, and listen to her children laugh.